D0916424

21 Days of Fasting
God's Way

Israel Hernández

Israel Hernández

Copyright © 2018 Matthew 10:32 Publishing All rights reserved.

King James Version

Photo Cover by Jeremy Yap on Unsplash
ISBN-10: 0-9862265-6-4
ISBN-13: 978-0-9862265-6-4
Edited by Carrie Hernandez

DEDICATION

TO MY LORD AND SAVIOR, JESUS

TO MY BELOVED WIFE AND COMPANION IN FAITH

TO MY SON NATHANAEL

TO BILL AND SANDY GERMAIN (MOM AND DAD)

Israel Hernández

Introduction

This book is a guide to show you how to fast for 21 days using Daniel's example. Before you start any fast, seek guidance from God. Don't make a decision to fast from emotions or simply accept an invitation from others. It is important to understand that fasting is not a diet. The purpose of this book is not to help you lose weight (although you probably will), but the point is to grow spiritually and get closer to God.

There are different kinds of fasting you can do. Only you and God can choose which one is best at any given time. It is very important during your fast that you focus on the spiritual not just on abstaining from food.

Here are some common forms of fasting:

- Do not eat anything, just drink water

- Do not eat anything, just drink juices
- Do not eat or drink anything (Jesus and Moses)
- Eat only fruits, vegetables and grains

There are people who use a physical condition as an excuse for not fasting, but you can always adjust the fast to meet your health needs. On the other hand you must remember that if it does not cost you anything then it is not a fast. Fasting is a sacrifice we make to subdue the flesh and connect with God. It is not only the sacrifice that moves God but our heart.

Before starting any fast, spend time in prayer and seek God to direct you as to what kind of fast you should choose and how long you should fast. Do not try to fast any more or less than God tells you. You must keep any promise you make to God.

I recommend that you start fasting on Sunday because it is good to start after attending church. It is good to ask for prayer for strength. Above all, I recommend that you invite other people to join the fast with you. It is easier when there are people praying for each other and supporting each other.

Note: The Bible Version used in the Biblical Reading of the day is King James Version. I recommend that you use the version that you most like.

Day 1

Fasting is a powerful weapon but it only works for Christians, for those who love the Lord. If you have never received Jesus in your heart, as Lord and Savior, and you have not been filled with the Holy Spirit, I invite you not to leave it until tomorrow.

Think of things you need to remove from your life or to breakthrough in the spiritual, such as anger, lust, a sense of loneliness, illness, alcoholism, relationships etc. Fasting is the best way to break sinful habits.

Make a daily plan. Include prayer, praise and devotions. Try to start first thing in the morning. Begin your day in prayer and finish it in prayer. On one of the fasting days I will teach you how to meditate on the Word and how to write devotionals.

Reading the Bible is crucial. We will include biblical passages to begin to create the habit of reading the Word of God daily.

As I do not know the spiritual life of all those who participate in fasting, I will include lessons on how to pray and how to listen to the voice of God.

The other thing that you should include in your fast is to substitute the time you normally dedicate to television, internet and social networks with time alone with God. There is nothing more important than spending time alone in prayer, worship and in the Word. You should plan to only watch Christian television and listen only to Christian music during the fast.

Prayer for Today

Lord, I thank You for this new opportunity to fast and to get closer to You. I ask You to be with me and support me. May Your Word be my bread and Your Spirit my peace. In the name of Jesus. Amen.

Biblical Reading of the Day

John 1:19-34

And this is the record of John, when the Jews sent priests and Levites from Jerusalem to ask him, Who art thou? And he confessed, and denied not; but confessed, I am not the Christ. And they asked him, What then? Art thou Elias? And he saith, I am not. Art thou that prophet? And he answered, No. Then said they unto him, Who art thou? that we may give an answer to them that sent us. What sayest thou of thyself? He said, I am the voice of one crying in the wilderness, Make straight the way of the Lord, as said the prophet Esaias. And they which were sent were of the Pharisees. And they asked him, and said unto him, Why baptizest thou then, if thou be not that Christ, nor Elias, neither that prophet? John answered them, saying, I baptize with water: but there standeth one among you, whom ye know not; He it is, who coming after me is preferred before me, whose shoe's latchet I am not worthy to unloose. These things were done in Bethabara beyond Jordan, where John was baptizing. The next day John seeth Jesus coming unto him, and saith, Behold the Lamb of God, which taketh away the sin of the world. This is he of whom I said, After me cometh a man which is preferred before me: for he was before me. And I knew him not: but that he should be made manifest to Israel, therefore am I come baptizing with water.

And John bare record, saying, I saw the Spirit descending from heaven like a dove, and it abode upon him. And I knew him not: but he that sent me to baptize with water, the same said unto me, Upon whom thou shalt see the Spirit descending, and remaining on him, the same is he which baptizeth with the Holy Ghost. And I saw, and bare record that this is the Son of God.
(John 1:19-34 KJV)

Devotional Day 1

Then he said to me, "Do not fear, Daniel, for from the first day that you set your heart to understand, and to humble yourself before your God, your words were heard; and I have come because of your words. But the prince of the kingdom of Persia withstood me twenty-one days; and behold, Michael, one of the chief princes, came to help me, for I had been left alone there with the kings of Persia. (Daniel 10:12-13 KJV)

Be Persistent in Prayer

Daniel was troubled by the future of his people. His answer was to humble himself before God in fasting and prayer for 21 days. Prayer was part Daniel's life. He always prayed three times a day. Daniel prayed and fasted for 21 days without receiving an answer from God, do you think he was discouraged when he didn't receive God's response during the fast?

Faithfully Daniel finished the fast that was chosen and in this passage we see why the answer to Daniel's prayer was delayed. Three days after the end of the fast the angel came to him. He told him that his prayer was heard from day one.

So God listens to you today. You may not see the answer today, not tomorrow, but surely God will answer you.

Perseverance in prayer was crucial in this scripture. If Daniel had become discouraged, frustrated or bitter, the angel would have had no reason to face the demon prince of Persia.

Be persistent in your fasting and prayer. The result will be glorious in all areas of your life, but especially in your spiritual life, which is the most important.

If you need prayer, we will always be available to pray for you.

Day 2

Moreover when ye fast, be not, as the hypocrites, of a sad countenance: for they disfigure their faces, that they may appear unto men to fast. Verily I say unto you, They have their reward. But thou, when thou fastest, anoint thine head, and wash thy face; That thou appear not unto men to fast, but unto thy Father which is in secret: and thy Father, which seeth in secret, shall reward thee openly.
(Matthew 6:16-18 KJV)

Fasting is something intimate between you and God. Not something that do with pride to impress others. There is nothing wrong with your co-workers or schoolmates discovering that you are fasting. Just let the moment come by itself, do not publish it to the four winds.

If you tend to eat frequently during your work hours or you are the one who always brings sweets or candy, people will realize that something is different. In those moments it is appropriate to tell them that you are fasting, if they ask you. You can avoid the temptation to eat or eat something that is not allowed in your fast when you do not have people offering you food all the time.

What Jesus is teaching us is that we should not publish the fast and put on sad and afflicted faces so that they may feel sorry for us. If nobody knows that you are fasting it's better. We do not want them to mock God because you decided to fast and now you walk as if you were starving. On the other hand we should not act as if we were more spiritual or stronger than others because we are fasting for 21 days.

The result of our fasting depends on our heart. The main reason for making this sacrifice is to be closer to our heavenly Father. Try to hide your fast as much as possible and when everyone is aware, take the opportunity to talk about Jesus and what He means to you.

Prayer for Today

Good morning dear Father. Thank You for this day that You have created. Thank You for giving me the great privilege of knowing You and experiencing Your immense love. Guide me during this day to where You want to take me. Fill my mind with thoughts that come from You. As I continue this fast, continue to strengthen me and encourage me to keep moving forward. In the name of Jesus. Amen.

Biblical Reading of the Day

John 4:1-42

When therefore the Lord knew how the Pharisees had heard that Jesus made and baptized more disciples than John, (Though Jesus himself baptized not, but his disciples,) He left Judaea, and departed again into Galilee. And he must needs go through Samaria. Then cometh he to a city of Samaria, which is called Sychar, near to the parcel of ground that Jacob gave to his son Joseph. Now Jacob's well was there. Jesus therefore, being wearied with his journey, sat thus on the well: and it was about the sixth hour. There cometh a woman of Samaria to draw water: Jesus saith unto her, Give me to drink. (For his disciples were gone away unto the city to buy meat.) Then saith the woman of Samaria unto him, How is it that thou, being a Jew, askest drink of me, which am a woman of Samaria? for the Jews have no dealings with the Samaritans. Jesus answered and said unto her, If thou knewest the gift of God, and who it is that saith to thee, Give me to drink; thou wouldest have asked of him, and he would have given thee living water. The woman saith unto him, Sir, thou hast nothing to draw with, and the well is deep: from whence then hast thou that living water? Art thou greater than our father Jacob, which gave us the well, and drank thereof himself, and his children, and his cattle? Jesus answered and said unto her, Whosoever drinketh of this water shall thirst again: But whosoever drinketh of the water that I shall give him shall never thirst; but the water that I shall give him shall be in him a well of water springing up into everlasting life. The woman saith unto him, Sir, give me this water, that I thirst not, neither come hither to draw. Jesus saith unto her, Go, call thy husband, and come hither. The woman answered and said, I have no husband. Jesus said unto her, Thou hast well said, I have no husband: For thou hast had five husbands; and he whom thou now hast is not thy husband: in that saidst thou truly. The woman saith unto him, Sir, I perceive that thou art a prophet. Our fathers worshipped in this mountain; and ye say, that in Jerusalem is the place where men ought to worship. Jesus saith unto her, Woman, believe me, the hour cometh, when ye shall neither in this mountain, nor yet at Jerusalem, worship the Father. Ye worship ye know not what: we know what we worship: for salvation is of the Jews. But the hour cometh, and now is, when the true worshippers shall worship the Father in spirit and in truth: for the Father seeketh such to worship him. God is a Spirit: and they that worship him must worship him in spirit and in truth. The woman saith unto him, I know that Messias cometh, which is called Christ: when he is come, he will tell us all things. Jesus saith unto her, I that speak unto thee am he. And upon this came his disciples, and marvelled that he talked with the woman: yet no man said, What seekest thou? or, Why talkest thou with her? The woman then left her waterpot, and went her way into the city, and saith to the men, Come, see a man, which told me all things that ever I did: is not this the Christ? Then they went out of the city, and came unto him. In the mean while his disciples prayed him, saying, Master, eat. But he said unto them, I have meat to eat that ye know not of. Therefore said the disciples one to another, Hath any man brought him ought to eat? Jesus saith unto them, My meat is to do the will of him that sent me, and to finish his work. Say not ye, There are yet four months, and then cometh harvest? behold, I say unto you, Lift up your eyes, and look on the fields; for they are white already to harvest. And he that reapeth receiveth wages, and gathereth fruit unto life eternal: that both he that soweth and he that reapeth may rejoice together. And herein is that saying true, One soweth, and another reapeth. I sent you to reap that whereon ye bestowed no labour: other men laboured, and ye are entered into their labours. And many of the Samaritans of that city believed on him for the saying of the woman, which testified, He told me all that ever I did. So when the Samaritans were come unto him, they besought him that he would tarry with them: and he abode there two days. And many more believed because of his own word; And said unto the woman, Now we believe, not because of thy saying: for we have heard him ourselves, and know that this is indeed the Christ, the Saviour of the world. (John 4:1-42 KJV)

Devotional Day 2

A Psalm of David, when he was in the wilderness of Judah. O God, thou art my God; early will I seek thee: my soul thirsteth for thee, my flesh longeth for thee in a dry and thirsty land, where no water is;
(Psalms 63:1 KJV)

In the morning I will seek God

Our Lord and Savior is always available. He always sees and listens to us no matter where you are or at what time you look for Him. But there is something special and even powerful when we seek God at dawn.

When we start the day seeking His face, His love and direction, we show Him how much we need Him and how much we love Him. Every morning when I get up, I tell my wife that I love her, I let her know how important she is to me. Now imagine that I get out of bed and start my day without acknowledging her. If I ignore her all morning and, maybe in the afternoon, I talk to her, how would she feel?

Likewise, God feels the same way. When we get up, we grab the phone to see the social networks, we take care of our to do list, and we do not recognize the One who loved us before He formed us. What if God did the same with us and "forgot" to love us, or to protect us from physical and spiritual dangers, until a moment is the afternoon when He finally remembered us.

Begin to acknowledge God in the morning. Talk to Him while you are still in bed and then seek Him in prayer. Make your Savior the priority of your day because we are His priority. Love shows when we dedicate quality time and make someone our priority.

Then was Jesus led up of the Spirit into the wilderness to be tempted of the devil. And when he had fasted forty days and forty nights, he was afterward an hungred. And when the tempter came to him, he said, If thou be the Son of God, command that these stones be made bread. But he answered and said, It is written, Man shall not live by bread alone, but by every word that proceedeth out of the mouth of God. (Matthew 4:1-4 KJV)

Today we will see the example of Jesus and His fast. The fast of Jesus consisted of forty days without eating or drinking just like the fast of Moses on Mt. Sinai. Those are the only "total" fasts recorded in the Bible. There is no call from God for the believer to imitate this type of fasting or number of days. These cases were special.

When Moses was in the presence of God, speaking face to

face with Him, he was sustained by God. He spent forty days receiving the commandments and the law of God. In the case of Jesus, He spent forty days alone in the desert and was tempted to break the same law that God gave Moses.

Notice how the Word says "He was led by the Spirit". The Holy Spirit is the One who directs us to fast and the One who sustains us. That's why I said at the beginning that you need to spend time alone with God and ask Him to direct this fasting. There must be a move or call from God to cope with the 21 days.

Take into account that Jesus was tempted almost at the end of His fast. The moment the devil chose was when He was hungry, when He was weaker. Do not be surprised if during the fast things start to go differently than planned. There is no guarantee that during the fast everything will go well. Fasting is a form of spiritual warfare.

The enemy of our souls tempted Jesus three times at the end of His fast. The three times our Savior overcame the temptations using the Word. "Man shall not live by bread alone, but by every Word that comes from the mouth of God." It was not something that Jesus invented at that moment but He recited Deuteronomy 8:3.

Begin to declare the Word to overcome temptations. There is no more powerful weapon to defeat the kingdom of darkness than by declaring and using the Sword of the Spirit that is the Word of God.

Prayer for Today

Heavenly Father, I know that You are always with me. Take me to the highest place, to Your presence. I need more of You because I am nothing if You are not by my side. Teach me to declare Your Word during the day to overcome every temptation that arises. I love You Lord. In the name of Jesus. Amen.

Biblical Reading of the Day

Matthew 5:1-20

And seeing the multitudes, he went up into a mountain: and when he was set, his disciples came unto him: And he opened his mouth, and taught them, saying, Blessed are the poor in spirit: for theirs is the kingdom of heaven. Blessed are they that mourn: for they shall be comforted. Blessed are the meek: for they shall inherit the earth. Blessed are they which do hunger and thirst after righteousness: for they shall be filled. Blessed are the merciful: for they shall obtain mercy. Blessed are the pure in heart: for they shall see God. Blessed are the peacemakers: for they shall be called the children of God. Blessed are they which are persecuted for righteousness' sake: for theirs is the kingdom of heaven. Blessed are ye, when men shall revile you, and persecute you, and shall say all manner of evil against you falsely, for my sake. Rejoice, and be exceeding glad: for great is your reward in heaven: for so persecuted they the prophets which were before you. Ye are the salt of the earth: but if the salt have lost his savour, wherewith shall it be salted? it is thenceforth good for nothing, but to be cast out, and to be trodden under foot of men. Ye are the light of the

world. A city that is set on an hill cannot be hid. Neither do men light a candle, and put it under a bushel, but on a candlestick; and it giveth light unto all that are in the house. Let your light so shine before men, that they may see your good works, and glorify your Father which is in heaven. Think not that I am come to destroy the law, or the prophets: I am not come to destroy, but to fulfil. For verily I say unto you, Till heaven and earth pass, one jot or one tittle shall in no wise pass from the law, till all be fulfilled. Whosoever therefore shall break one of these least commandments, and shall teach men so, he shall be called the least in the kingdom of heaven: but whosoever shall do and teach them, the same shall be called great in the kingdom of heaven. For I say unto you, That except your righteousness shall exceed the righteousness of the scribes and Pharisees, ye shall in no case enter into the kingdom of heaven.
(Matthew 5:1-20 KJV)

Devotional Day 3

A Psalm or Song for the sabbath day. It is a good thing to give thanks unto the LORD, and to sing praises unto thy name, O most High: To shew forth thy lovingkindness in the morning, and thy faithfulness every night,
(Psalms 92:1-2 KJV)

It is good to praise God

Praise is an action that comes out of our spirit. God rejoices when from deep within us we bring out a song of praise and adoration. Not only when we are in victory, but at all times.

Praise God in the trial, recognizing that He is with you and is on your side. What you are going through at this moment is not permanent, you will break through to the other side. And when you succeed, sing a hymn of victory to the Lord.

It is important to sing songs of praise to the Lord during fasting. Just as a woman falls in love when the gentleman dedicates romantic songs to her. Fall in love with Jesus and sing to Him, "I long for you, I need you, I love you". He alone is worthy of praise.

Day 4

Do not give up!

You are already on day 4 of the 21-day fast. The worst days are the first 3. The body is already accustomed to the dietary adjustments. Remember that this is not a diet but a spiritual fast, so God is on your side.

Keep the goal in mind all the times. I know it's hard for some people, especially if it's your first time. Maybe it's time to adjust your fast depending on what God asked you to do. It is not good to break what you promised to God but also God understands your weakness. He can give you strength.

You must not stop but keep moving forward. Yesterday we learned to declare the Word "Man shall not live by bread alone, but by every Word that comes from the mouth of God." There are many biblical verses that we can declare during the fast.

... let the weak say I am strong.
Joel 3:10

I can do all things through Christ who strengthens me.
Philippians 4:13

Keep going! What you should not change is your time alone with God. That should increase! Time reading the Word, meditating on the Word, praising and worshiping and praying should not diminish. The most important thing is your spiritual connection.

If you have difficulty coping with the fast now or at any time, do not hesitate to contact us through the email contacto@mcajesus.com

Prayer for Today

Thank You God for this season and for the opportunity to begin it in fasting and prayer. Thank You for this day and for what I have learned in Your Word. Thank you for always being by my side. In the name of Jesus. Amen.

Biblical Reading of the Day

Luke 4:14-41

And Jesus returned in the power of the Spirit into Galilee: and there went out a fame of him through all the region round about. And he taught in their synagogues, being glorified of all. And he came to Nazareth, where he had been brought up: and, as his custom was, he went into the synagogue on the sabbath day, and stood up for to read. And there was delivered unto him the book of the prophet Esaias. And when he had opened the book, he found the place where it was written, The Spirit of the Lord is upon me, because he hath anointed me to preach the gospel to the poor; he hath sent me to heal the brokenhearted, to preach deliverance to the captives, and recovering of sight to the blind, to set at liberty them that are bruised, To preach the acceptable year of the Lord. And he closed the book, and he gave it again to the minister, and sat down. And the eyes of all them that were in the synagogue were fastened on him. And he began to say unto them, This day is this scripture fulfilled in your ears. And all bare him witness, and wondered at the gracious words which proceeded out of his mouth. And they said, Is not this Joseph's son? And he said unto them, Ye will surely say unto me this proverb, Physician, heal thyself: whatsoever we have heard done in Capernaum, do also here in thy country. And he said, Verily I say unto you, No prophet is accepted in his own country. But I tell you of a truth, many widows were in Israel in the days of Elias, when the heaven was shut up three years and six months, when great famine was throughout all the land; But unto none of them was Elias sent, save unto Sarepta, a city of Sidon, unto a woman that was a widow. And many lepers were in Israel in the time of Eliseus the prophet; and none of them was cleansed, saving Naaman the Syrian. And all they in the synagogue, when they heard these things, were filled with wrath, And rose up, and thrust him out of the city, and led him unto the brow of the hill whereon their city was built, that they might cast him down headlong. But he passing through the midst of them went his way, And came down to Capernaum, a city of Galilee, and taught them on the sabbath days. And they were astonished at his doctrine: for his word was with power. And in the synagogue there was a man, which had a spirit of an unclean devil, and cried out with a loud voice, Saying, Let us alone; what have we to do with thee, thou Jesus of Nazareth? art thou come to destroy us? I know thee who thou art; the Holy One of God. And Jesus rebuked him, saying, Hold thy peace, and come out of him. And when the devil had thrown him in the midst, he came out of him, and hurt him not. And they were all amazed, and spake among themselves, saying, What a word is this! for with authority and power he commandeth the unclean spirits, and they come out. And the fame of him went out into every place of the country round about. And he arose out of the synagogue, and entered into Simon's house. And Simon's wife's mother was taken with a great fever; and they besought him for her. And he stood over her, and rebuked the fever;

and it left her: and immediately she arose and ministered unto them. Now when the sun was setting, all they that had any sick with divers diseases brought them unto him; and he laid his hands on every one of them, and healed them. And devils also came out of many, crying out, and saying, Thou art Christ the Son of God. And he rebuking them suffered them not to speak: for they knew that he was Christ. (Luke 4:14-41 KJV)

Devotional Day 4

As they ministered to the Lord, and fasted, the Holy Ghost said, Separate me Barnabas and Saul for the work whereunto I have called them. And when they had fasted and prayed, and laid their hands on them, they sent them away.

(Acts 13:2-3 KJV)

When you fast the Holy Spirit speaks to you

The Holy Spirit that dwells in everyone who has been born again is always talking to us. But for many it is difficult to hear and understand what God is saying.

When we fast, we become more filled with Jesus, spending more time alone with Him, meditating on His Word, and communicating with Him in prayer. These are all things we should already be doing daily but they should be intensified during the fast.

Our spirit is more willing and our spiritual ears are more sensitive. It is the best time to receive guidance from God. The apostles experienced that frequently because they maintained a life of fasting and prayer.

Not only did they receive God's direction to send Barnabas

and Paul during the fast but they fasted again to strengthen them in their spirit and send them to the work of God. Prepare your spiritual ears to receive guidance from the Holy Spirit. Fill yourself with God.

Day 5

But they that wait upon the LORD shall renew their strength; they shall mount up with wings as eagles; they shall run, and not be weary; and they shall walk, and not faint.
(Isaiah 40:31 KJV)

Your strength comes from God

He will strengthen you when you do not have strength. Wait on Him and give the Lord the best you can. Our heavenly Father sees the intentions of the heart and even our thoughts. He knows your intentions and what motivates you to perform this fast.

What God will do with you at the end of the fast will be glorious and the changes will be noticed by everyone around you. Right now, after 4 days fasting and praying, you should feel closer to God.

Today decide to perform an act of mercy for someone you

do not know. Show the love that God has placed in you. Regardless of the consequences or the reaction of others, when we perform an act of mercy for someone who cannot pay us back, we show that Jesus lives in us.

If you feel tired and exhausted, wait on the Lord. Do not be discouraged but use the opportunity to prove that God's promises are true and always will be true.

Prayer for Today

Lord, I recognize that I need You and outside of You I can do nothing. Thank You for giving me the strength to continue this fast. Help me to walk in mercy with others and to be more like You. I love You Lord. In the name of Jesus. Amen.

Biblical Reading of the Day

1 John 1:1-10

That which was from the beginning, which we have heard, which we have seen with our eyes, which we have looked upon, and our hands have handled, of the Word of life; (For the life was manifested, and we have seen it, and bear witness, and shew unto you that eternal life, which was with the Father, and was manifested unto us;) That which we have seen and heard declare we unto you, that ye also may have fellowship with us: and truly our fellowship is with the Father, and with his Son Jesus Christ. And these things write we unto you, that your joy may be full. This then is the message which we have heard of him, and declare unto you, that God is light, and in him is no darkness at all. If we say that we have fellowship with him, and walk in darkness, we lie, and do not the truth: But if we walk in the light, as he is in the light, we have fellowship one with another, and the blood of Jesus Christ his Son cleanseth us from all sin. If we say that we have no sin, we deceive ourselves, and the truth is not in us. If we confess our sins, he is faithful and just to forgive us our sins, and to cleanse us from all unrighteousness. If we say that we have not sinned, we make him a liar, and his word is not in us.
(1 John 1:1-10 KJV)

Devotional Day 5

**And king David said to Ornan, Nay; but I will verily buy it for the full price: for I will not take that which is thine for the LORD, nor offer burnt offerings without cost.
(1 Chronicles 21:24 KJV)**

God is given the best

The sacrifice we make to get closer to God is seen by our heavenly Father and will be rewarded. It is not an act of manipulation to get something in return but, when we do it from the heart, God will bless us.

I do not mean vain sacrifices like repeating the same prayer ten times a day or walking on your knees. If we do not have a clean and pure heart, our sacrifice is worth nothing.

Do not give God the crumbs. This is what this scripture teaches us. The king could take the field for free but that would not please the Lord. If we love God we have to give Him the best we can. If what you give to God has no value then do not expect God to move in your favor.

Check the intentions that motivated you to begin this fast. Think about what you are eating, is it a sacrifice? What time do you dedicate to being alone with God? What things do you do besides pray and spend time with God during the fast? How do you treat others?

Today is Friday!

Yes, the weekend is here and you have already completed 6 days. The Lord is seeing your commitment to Him and will continue to sustain you until the 21st day. At this time your body should be adjusted to your fast.

Now is the time to increase your time alone with God a little. It is what pleases God the most after obedience. The sense of closeness to God is greater than when we started.

If you are tired and you are tempted to break the fast, look for someone to support you. Maybe someone you know who is participating in the fast can be a good partner. You can also invite others to join.

Something we have to practice during any fast is kindly saying "NO". When they offer us food, they invite us to eat or go out for a walk, saying "NO" in a nice way will help us to continue to establish our relationship with God first.

Prayer for Today

My beloved Father, thank You for guiding me and strengthening me. I know You will be with me all the way and I look forward to finishing the fast in its entirety. But I also know that temptations come and what I want is to please You. Help me not to give up. In the name of Jesus. Amen.

Biblical Reading of the Day

Psalm 91: 1-16

He that dwelleth in the secret place of the most High shall abide under the shadow of the Almighty. I will say of the LORD, He is my refuge and my fortress: my God; in him will I trust. Surely he shall deliver thee from the snare of the fowler, and from the noisome pestilence. He shall cover thee with his feathers, and under his wings shalt thou trust: his truth shall be thy shield and buckler. Thou shalt not be afraid for the terror by night; nor for the arrow that flieth by day; Nor for the pestilence that walketh in darkness; nor for the destruction that wasteth at noonday. A thousand shall fall at thy side, and ten thousand at thy right hand; but it shall not come nigh thee. Only with thine eyes shalt thou behold and see the reward of the wicked. Because thou hast made the LORD, which is my refuge, even the most High, thy habitation; There shall no evil befall thee, neither shall any plague come nigh thy dwelling. For he shall give his angels charge over thee, to keep thee in all thy ways. They shall bear thee up in their hands, lest thou dash thy foot against a stone. Thou shalt tread upon the lion and adder: the young lion and the dragon shalt thou trample under feet. Because he hath set

his love upon me, therefore will I deliver him: I will set him on high, because he hath known my name. He shall call upon me, and I will answer him: I will be with him in trouble; I will deliver him, and honour him. With long life will I satisfy him, and shew him my salvation.
(Psalms 91:1-16 KJV)

Devotional Day 6

Be ye therefore followers of God, as dear children; And walk in love, as Christ also hath loved us, and hath given himself for us an offering and a sacrifice to God for a sweetsmelling savour. (Ephesians 5:1-2 KJV)

Imitate Jesus and you will be on the right path

Jesus walked among us with an unblemished record. Evil was never found in Him because He never sinned. His love and mercy for the needy was what motivated Him.

Now, we Christians who are born again, we are not only called to worship and serve Jesus, but we have to imitate Him.

How much do you look like Jesus? While we're on this earth we can never be perfect images of Jesus but we can resemble Him. Our goal should be to speak as He spoke, walk as He walked, pray as He prayed and do all He did.

Fasting and prayer is part of imitating what Jesus did. That includes serving the needy, putting the will of the Father first and giving your life for others. We do not have to be the best we can be, we have to be more like Jesus.

Day 7

The Lord is smiling at you

Despite how difficult this week has been, today you have reached the 7th day of your fast. Surely temptations came, people offered you food that you have given up. Maybe you stumbled for a moment during the week and you feel guilty.

The important thing is that you are still on the path to victory. Keep walking. Fasting is not only not eating but it is a way to humble yourself before God with a broken and repentant heart. Present your sins before God every day and those of your family. Remember that if we do not have a clean heart, nothing we do will be worth anything. Love and mercy are the first things that God wants to see in us, and then sacrifices.

Finish strong this first week, prepare to make the food adjustments that you already promised to the Lord. Do not break the promises you made to God. But you can pray and ask God to guide you in a new plan for the next two weeks.

What should not have changed is your time with God, time reading the scriptures and worship. The spiritual connection with your heavenly Father is what will change you from the inside out. Be strong in the Lord!

Prayer for Today

Our Father, thank You for this first week of fasting. You have sustained me with Your powerful hand and Your arms of love. I want to be closer to You every day. Help me to walk in Your love and share it with others. In the name of Jesus. Amen.

Biblical Reading of the Day

Ephesians 5:1-33

Be ye therefore followers of God, as dear children; And walk in love, as Christ also hath loved us, and hath given himself for us an offering and a sacrifice to God for a sweetsmelling savour. But fornication, and all uncleanness, or covetousness, let it not be once named among you, as becometh saints; Neither filthiness, nor foolish talking, nor jesting, which are not convenient: but rather giving of thanks. For this ye know, that no whoremonger, nor unclean person, nor covetous man, who is an idolater, hath any inheritance in the kingdom of Christ and of God. Let no man deceive you with vain words: for because of these things cometh the wrath of God upon the children of disobedience. Be not ye therefore partakers with them. For ye were sometimes darkness, but now are ye light in the Lord: walk as children of light: (For the fruit of the Spirit is in all goodness and righteousness and truth;) Proving what is acceptable unto the Lord. And have no fellowship with the unfruitful works of darkness, but rather reprove them. For it is a shame even to speak of those things which are done of them in secret. But all things that are reproved are made manifest by the light: for whatsoever doth make manifest is light. Wherefore he saith, Awake thou that sleepest, and arise from the dead, and Christ shall give thee light. See then that ye walk circumspectly, not as fools, but as wise, Redeeming the time, because the days are evil. Wherefore be ye not unwise, but understanding what the will of the Lord is. And be not drunk with wine, wherein is excess; but be filled with the Spirit; Speaking to yourselves in psalms and hymns and spiritual songs, singing and making melody in your heart to the Lord; Giving thanks always for all things unto God and the Father in the name of our Lord Jesus Christ; Submitting yourselves one to another in the fear of God. Wives, submit yourselves unto your own husbands, as unto the Lord. For the husband is the head of the wife, even as Christ is the head of the church: and he is the saviour of the body. Therefore as the church is subject unto Christ, so let the wives be to their own husbands in every thing. Husbands, love your wives, even as Christ also loved the church, and gave himself for it; That he might sanctify and cleanse it with the washing of water by the word, That he might present it to himself a glorious church, not having spot, or wrinkle, or any such thing; but that it should be holy and without blemish. So ought men to love their wives as their own bodies. He that loveth his wife loveth himself. For no man ever yet hated his own flesh; but nourisheth and cherisheth it, even as the Lord the church: For we are members of his body, of his flesh, and of his bones. For this cause shall a man leave his father and mother, and shall be joined unto his wife, and they two shall be one flesh. This is a great mystery: but I speak concerning Christ and the church. Nevertheless let every one of you in particular so love his wife even as himself; and the wife see that she reverence her husband.

(Ephesians 5:1-33 KJV)

Devotional Day 7

I am the vine, ye are the branches: He that abideth in me, and I in him, the same bringeth forth much fruit: for without me ye can do nothing.
(John 15:5 KJV)

Remain in Him

Normally when we participate in a fast we feel very close to God. Our mind remains on the things of the Lord. The peace of God feels deeper than we have felt in a long time, but when the fast ends, do we remain in Him?

It is easy to fall into the things of the world when we stop doing what pleases God. Praying daily, reading the Bible every day and listening to only Christian music is not just something we do during a fast, but it is the lifestyle of the believer.

We want the blessings that come from fasting to last throughout the year but we don't want to continue dedicating our time to Him. Every fruit we bear comes from Him, we can do nothing without our Savior. Fasting is to recharge our spirit and returns us to doing what we should do. The only thing you should do different after fasting is to eat.

Israel Hernández

Separate this day for the Lord

The second week of fasting begins today. Dedicate this day to the Lord and seek His face. Go to church, receive the Word of God, worship with songs, and fellowship with other believers. The Lord can speak directly to you during the service, keep your spiritual ears open.

When you arrive home, spend the rest of the day in prayer, present your requests to God. Thank Him for everything He has done in your life. Intercede in prayer for your family. Pray that those who still do not know Jesus come to know Him.

The reading of the Word will be your delight. Spend a lot of time reading and meditating on the Word during the day. If there are other people in your house, share what you read with them and talk with them about what the scripture means.

Let the Holy Spirit fill you by spending time doing nothing but worshiping and praising our Lord. The God who dwells in the praise of His people will visit you during worship. He deserves all the praise, glory, and honor. Even more He rejoices in you when you wait on Him.

Prayer for Today

Dear Father, I thank You for this day that You have created for me to rejoice in. Your love and Your kindness are immense. Help me not to distract myself today with things that do not honor You. I want to walk with You Lord. In the name of Jesus. Amen.

Biblical Reading of the Day

Mark 3:1-35

And he entered again into the synagogue; and there was a man there which had a withered hand. And they watched him, whether he would heal him on the sabbath day; that they might accuse him. And he saith unto the man which had the withered hand, Stand forth. And he saith unto them, Is it lawful to do good on the sabbath days, or to do evil? to save life, or to kill? But they held their peace. And when he had looked round about on them with anger, being grieved for the hardness of their hearts, he saith unto the man, Stretch forth thine hand. And he stretched it out: and his hand was restored whole as the other. And the Pharisees went forth, and straightway took counsel with the Herodians against him, how they might destroy him. But Jesus withdrew himself with his disciples to the sea: and a great multitude from Galilee followed him, and from Judaea, And from Jerusalem, and from Idumaea, and from beyond Jordan; and they about Tyre and Sidon, a great multitude, when they had heard what great things he did, came unto him. And he spake to his disciples, that a small ship should wait on him because of the multitude, lest they should throng him. For he had healed many; insomuch that they pressed upon him for to touch him, as many as had plagues. And unclean spirits, when they saw him, fell down before him, and cried, saying, Thou art the Son of God. And he straitly charged them that they should not make him known. And he goeth up into a mountain, and calleth unto him whom he would: and they came unto him. And he ordained twelve, that they should be with him, and that he might send them forth to preach, And to have power to heal sicknesses, and to cast out devils: And Simon he surnamed Peter; And James the son of Zebedee, and John the brother of James; and he surnamed them Boanerges, which is, The sons of thunder: And Andrew, and Philip, and Bartholomew, and Matthew, and Thomas, and James the son of Alphaeus, and Thaddaeus, and Simon the Canaanite, And Judas Iscariot, which also betrayed him: and they went into an house. And the multitude cometh together again, so that they could not so much as eat bread. And when his friends heard of it, they went out to lay hold on him: for they said, He is beside himself. And the scribes which came down from Jerusalem said, He hath Beelzebub, and by the prince of the devils casteth he out devils. And he called them unto him, and said unto them in parables, How can Satan cast out Satan? And if a kingdom be divided against itself, that kingdom cannot stand. And if a house be divided against itself, that house cannot stand. And if Satan rise up against himself, and be divided, he cannot stand, but hath an end. No man can enter into a strong man's house, and spoil his goods, except he will first bind the strong man; and then he will spoil his house. Verily I say unto you, All sins shall be forgiven unto the sons of men, and blasphemies wherewith soever they shall blaspheme: But he that shall blaspheme against the Holy Ghost hath never forgiveness, but is in danger of eternal damnation: Because they said, He hath an

unclean spirit. There came then his brethren and his mother, and, standing without, sent unto him, calling him. And the multitude sat about him, and they said unto him, Behold, thy mother and thy brethren without seek for thee. And he answered them, saying, Who is my mother, or my brethren? And he looked round about on them which sat about him, and said, Behold my mother and my brethren! For whosoever shall do the will of God, the same is my brother, and my sister, and mother.
(Mark 3:1-35 KJV)

Devotional Day 8

And when he had sent the multitudes away, he went up into a mountain apart to pray: and when the evening was come, he was there alone. (Matthew 14:23 KJV)

Get away and get closer

Our Lord Jesus had the need to communicate with the Father at all times. Because Jesus was God and man at the same time, the relationship between God (Father, Son, and Holy Spirit) had to be maintained. Jesus, lived as an example for us and showed us how humans should relate to God.

It is very good to pray in the church, and it is good when we pray with other brothers and sisters in Christ. But it is imperative that we also separate ourselves and spend time alone with God.

In that time alone we can really open our hearts to the Father. We can be totally honest without worrying about what others will say. Set aside a place in your home, where no one will interrupt you, so you can spend time with God.

Intimacy with Jesus allows us to know Him better, and each day become more like Him. This must be something daily and constant. The place, whether in a room, bathroom, basement or car, is not as important as the quality time you give to the Lord. Jesus wants to spend time with you.

Day 9

I will speak of thy testimonies also before kings,
and will not be ashamed.
(Psalms 119:46 KJV)

Get up and preach!

The Lord has led you along the path during this fast and you are growing in spirit and in knowledge. The Word becomes more alive when you depend on God and dedicate days to walk with Him.

Now that you are full of the Word, share it with others. Talk about what you have learned, about the changes that the Lord has made in your life, and all that it means to love God and be loved by Him.

When something new comes into your life, especially something materially valuable, you share it with others with excitement. Sometimes you spend days talking about that thing. Why not talk about the most valuable thing you have?

Our salvation in Jesus Christ is the most valuable thing that we have and that we can ever have. When it's combined with the joy of having eternal life our excitement produces a deep passion to preach to others. Who do you think will speak to your relatives and companions about Jesus?

The limitations for me to preach to your friends and family are great as are the limitations for the pastors in your area to do so. It is necessary that we do the work that is most important to Jesus, which is to save all those who want to be saved. The desire of God is that everyone has an eternal dwelling with Him, and you are an instrument to achieve this. Get up and preach!

Prayer for Today

Lord, I thank You because You sent Your son Jesus, so I could be saved. Help me to share that salvation with those who are close to me, especially my relatives who do not know You. I ask You in the name of Jesus. Amen.

Biblical Reading of the Day

Acts 8:1-40

And Saul was consenting unto his death. And at that time there was a great persecution against the church which was at Jerusalem; and they were all scattered abroad throughout the regions of Judaea and Samaria, except the apostles. And devout men carried Stephen to his burial, and made great lamentation over him. As for Saul, he made havock of the church, entering into every house, and haling men and women committed them to prison. Therefore they that were scattered abroad went every where preaching the word. Then Philip went down to the city of Samaria, and preached Christ unto them. And the people with one accord gave heed unto those things which Philip spake, hearing and seeing the miracles which he did. For unclean spirits, crying with loud voice, came out of many that were possessed with them: and many taken with palsies, and that were lame, were healed. And there was great joy in that city. But there was a certain man, called Simon, which beforetime in the same city used sorcery, and bewitched the people of Samaria, giving out that himself was some great one: To whom they all gave heed, from the least to the greatest, saying, This man is the great power of God. And to him they had regard, because that of long time he had bewitched them with sorceries. But when they believed Philip preaching the things concerning the kingdom of God, and the name of Jesus Christ, they were baptized, both men and women. Then Simon himself believed also: and when he was baptized, he continued with Philip, and wondered, beholding the miracles and signs which were done. Now when the apostles which were at Jerusalem heard that Samaria had received the word of God, they sent unto them Peter and John: Who, when they were come down, prayed for them, that they might receive the Holy Ghost: (For as yet he was fallen upon none of them: only they were baptized in the name of the Lord Jesus.) Then laid they their hands on them, and they received the Holy Ghost. And when Simon saw that through laying on of the apostles' hands the Holy Ghost was given, he offered them money, Saying, Give me also this power, that on whomsoever I lay hands, he may receive the Holy Ghost. But Peter said unto him, Thy money perish with thee, because thou hast thought that the gift of God may be purchased with money. Thou hast neither part nor lot in this matter: for thy heart is not right in the sight of God. Repent therefore of this thy wickedness, and pray God, if perhaps the thought of thine heart may be forgiven thee. For I perceive that thou art in the gall of bitterness, and in the bond of iniquity. Then answered Simon, and said, Pray ye to the Lord for me, that none of these things which ye have spoken come upon me. And they, when they had testified and preached the word of the Lord, returned to Jerusalem, and preached the gospel in many villages of the Samaritans. And the angel of the Lord spake unto Philip, saying, Arise, and go toward the south unto the way that goeth down from Jerusalem unto Gaza, which is desert. And he arose and went: and, behold, a man

of Ethiopia, an eunuch of great authority under Candace queen of the Ethiopians, who had the charge of all her treasure, and had come to Jerusalem for to worship, Was returning, and sitting in his chariot read Esaias the prophet. Then the Spirit said unto Philip, Go near, and join thyself to this chariot. And Philip ran thither to him, and heard him read the prophet Esaias, and said, Understandest thou what thou readest? And he said, How can I, except some man should guide me? And he desired Philip that he would come up and sit with him. The place of the scripture which he read was this, He was led as a sheep to the slaughter; and like a lamb dumb before his shearer, so opened he not his mouth: In his humiliation his judgment was taken away: and who shall declare his generation? for his life is taken from the earth. And the eunuch answered Philip, and said, I pray thee, of whom speaketh the prophet this? of himself, or of some other man? Then Philip opened his mouth, and began at the same scripture, and preached unto him Jesus. And as they went on their way, they came unto a certain water: and the eunuch said, See, here is water; what doth hinder me to be baptized? And Philip said, If thou believest with all thine heart, thou mayest. And he answered and said, I believe that Jesus Christ is the Son of God. And he commanded the chariot to stand still: and they went down both into the water, both Philip and the eunuch; and he baptized him. And when they were come up out of the water, the Spirit of the Lord caught away Philip, that the eunuch saw him no more: and he went on his way rejoicing. But Philip was found at Azotus: and passing through he preached in all the cities, till he came to Caesarea.
(Acts 8:1-40 KJV)

Devotional Day 9

If ye abide in me, and my words abide in you, ye shall ask what ye will, and it shall be done unto you.
(John 15:7 KJV)

Ask what you want!

Jesus invites us to ask for what we want. So what will you ask for? That car you've seen for months and cannot afford or a big house with more rooms than you can ever fill? Do not let your heart, or a prosperity pastor, cause you to deviate from what Jesus says. That is not what Jesus meant when He said He would provide everything you need according to His riches in glory.

To be able to ask for what you want, you have to remain in Him and in His Word. Spend time in prayer and worship. Spend time alone with Jesus daily in your prayer room and during the day. Keep Him on your mind.

Staying in His Word is reading it every day and obeying it. Take time to meditate on the scriptures and asking the Holy Spirit to teach you what they mean. Ask Him to help you to obey in love.

Then your heart will be ready to ask whatever you want because God will put desires in your heart that align with the will of God. Seek first the kingdom of God and His righteousness and everything else will be added to you.

I am crucified with Christ: nevertheless I live; yet not I, but Christ liveth in me: and the life which I now live in the flesh I live by the faith of the Son of God, who loved me, and gave himself for me. (Galatians 2:20 KJV)

Who lives in you?

Now that fasting is part of your daily life your heart is more open to receiving guidance from the Holy Spirit. Dying to our old life we press closer to the goal. What we live, we live in Christ Jesus.

If Christ really lives in me, the fruits of it have to be easily seen by others. That's why it's important to maintain the relationship with God that you have in this moment, even after the fast is over.

We learned that men will not live by bread alone but by every Word that comes from the mouth of God. So we must stay in the Word of God each day of our lives. The source of life for every believer is to eat from God's Bread of Life.

Jesus dwells in us, that is, He lives in us. We have to be more like Him and less like us. If He died for us, let us live for Him

Prayer for Today

Holy Father, thank You for this day and for helping me to focus on You. Forgive the times I've forgotten about You and forgotten to spend time with You. Since You live in me, help me to be more like You. In the name of Jesus. Amen.

Biblical Reading of the Day

Romans 8:1-39

There is therefore now no condemnation to them which are in Christ Jesus, who walk not after the flesh, but after the Spirit. For the law of the Spirit of life in Christ Jesus hath made me free from the law of sin and death. For what the law could not do, in that it was weak through the flesh, God sending his own Son in the likeness of sinful flesh, and for sin, condemned sin in the flesh: That the righteousness of the law might be fulfilled in us, who walk not after the flesh, but after the Spirit. For they that are after the flesh do mind the things of the flesh; but they that are after the Spirit the things of the Spirit. For to be carnally minded is death; but to be spiritually minded is life and peace. Because the carnal mind is enmity against God: for it is not subject to the law of God, neither indeed can be. So then they that are in the flesh cannot please God. But ye are not in the flesh, but in the Spirit, if so be that the Spirit of God dwell in you. Now if any man have not the Spirit of Christ, he is none of his. And if Christ be in you, the body is dead because of sin; but the Spirit is life because of righteousness. But if the Spirit of him that raised up Jesus from the dead dwell in you, he that raised up Christ from the dead shall also quicken your mortal bodies by his Spirit that dwelleth in you. Therefore, brethren, we are debtors, not to the flesh, to live after the flesh. For if ye live after the flesh, ye shall die: but if ye through the Spirit do mortify the deeds of the body, ye shall live. For as many as are led by the Spirit of God, they are the sons of God. For ye have not received the spirit of bondage again to fear; but ye have received the Spirit of adoption, whereby we cry, Abba, Father. The Spirit itself beareth witness with our spirit, that we are the children of God: And if children, then heirs; heirs of God, and joint-heirs with Christ; if so be that we suffer with him, that we may be also glorified together. For I reckon that the sufferings of this present time are not worthy to be compared with the glory which shall be revealed in us. For the earnest expectation of the creature waiteth for the manifestation of the sons of God. For the creature was made subject to vanity, not willingly, but by reason of him who hath subjected the same in hope, Because the creature itself also shall be delivered from the bondage of corruption into the glorious liberty of the children of God. For we know that the whole creation groaneth and travaileth in pain together until now. And not only they, but ourselves also, which have the firstfruits of the Spirit, even we ourselves groan within ourselves, waiting for the adoption, to wit, the redemption of our body. For we are saved by hope: but hope that is seen is not hope: for what a man seeth, why doth he yet hope for? But if we hope for that we see not, then do we with patience wait for it. Likewise the Spirit also helpeth our infirmities: for we know not what we should pray for as we ought: but the Spirit itself maketh intercession for us with groanings which cannot be uttered. And he that searcheth the hearts knoweth what is the mind of the Spirit, because he maketh

intercession for the saints according to the will of God. And we know that all things work together for good to them that love God, to them who are the called according to his purpose. For whom he did foreknow, he also did predestinate to be conformed to the image of his Son, that he might be the firstborn among many brethren. Moreover whom he did predestinate, them he also called: and whom he called, them he also justified: and whom he justified, them he also glorified. What shall we then say to these things? If God be for us, who can be against us? He that spared not his own Son, but delivered him up for us all, how shall he not with him also freely give us all things? Who shall lay any thing to the charge of God's elect? It is God that justifieth. Who is he that condemneth? It is Christ that died, yea rather, that is risen again, who is even at the right hand of God, who also maketh intercession for us. Who shall separate us from the love of Christ? shall tribulation, or distress, or persecution, or famine, or nakedness, or peril, or sword? As it is written, For thy sake we are killed all the day long; we are accounted as sheep for the slaughter. Nay, in all these things we are more than conquerors through him that loved us. For I am persuaded, that neither death, nor life, nor angels, nor principalities, nor powers, nor things present, nor things to come, Nor height, nor depth, nor any other creature, shall be able to separate us from the love of God, which is in Christ Jesus our Lord.
(Romans 8:1-39 KJV)

Devotional Day 10

This book of the law shall not depart out of thy mouth; but thou shalt meditate therein day and night, that thou mayest observe to do according to all that is written therein: for then thou shalt make thy way prosperous, and then thou shalt have good success.
(Joshua 1:8 KJV)

Meditating on the Word

Today we will learn to meditate on the Word and to write a devotional. Reading the Word and meditating on it are two different things. Reading is very important because it allows us to know what God is telling us and we can see how God operates.

Meditating on the Word is more than reading. It is scrutinizing the Word in order to understand what God did and how we can apply it in our lives. Meditating is learning to listen to the voice of God. We discover something new every time we meditate on the Word.

Now, before reading the Bible, pray to the Father to help you find the scripture that He wants you to meditate on. Then when you find that scripture something in you (The Holy Spirit) will let you know that you have found it. Then read that portion several times and ask the Lord to help you understand what He is saying to you and how to apply it to your life.

Write down what the Lord says to you, read it throughout the day, and share it with someone. Spending time reading the scripture and devotional He gives to you is a way of meditating on the Word day and night.

Day 11

Everything is going well

The sacrifice we make when we fast is different for each person but it has to cost us something to move God. There are people who are vegetarians and for them to do Daniel's fast would not be difficult at all. But for those who are accustomed to eating animal products it is more difficult.

Everything you do for the Lord with sacrifice and a clean heart will be rewarded. Surely your body will be healthier, because it is proven that fasting can reverse many diseases, if done properly.

You are already more than halfway done with your 21-day fast. You must be happy and proud that God has helped you and sustained you until now. In the days that are left, He will also sustain you, if you remain in Him.

Do not stop at this point, I know that some have broken their promise to God and have eaten something they gave up. Just ask the Lord for forgiveness and ask Him to help you to replace the days you failed. Do not condemn yourself, everything is fine, just keep walking.

The most important thing is not to give up. At this stage, pray more, spend more time alone with Jesus, and be sure that what you listen to is only Christian music. God has broken many of the bad and sinful habits of your past. You do not have to return to them if you remain in Him. In Him you are safe.

Prayer for Today

Lord, this day I thank You because looking back it seemed impossible to fast, but Your Word has been my food. Thanks for being so good. Help me to remain in You during the rest of this fast and all the days of my life. In the name of Jesus. Amen.

Biblical Reading of the Day

Psalm 27:1-14

A Psalm of David. The LORD is my light and my salvation; whom shall I fear? the LORD is the strength of my life; of whom shall I be afraid? When the wicked, even mine enemies and my foes, came upon me to eat up my flesh, they stumbled and fell. Though an host should encamp against me, my heart shall not fear: though war should rise against me, in this will I be confident. One thing have I desired of the LORD, that will I seek after; that I may dwell in the house of the LORD all the days of my life, to behold the beauty of the LORD, and to enquire in his temple. For in the time of trouble he shall hide me in his pavilion: in the secret of his tabernacle shall he hide me; he shall set me up upon a rock. And now shall mine head be lifted up above mine enemies round about me: therefore will I offer in his tabernacle sacrifices of joy; I will sing, yea, I will sing praises unto the LORD. Hear, O LORD, when I cry with my voice: have mercy also upon me, and answer me. When thou saidst, Seek ye my face; my heart said unto thee, Thy face, LORD, will I seek. Hide not thy face far from me; put not thy servant away in anger: thou hast been my help; leave me not, neither

forsake me, O God of my salvation. When my father and my mother forsake me, then the LORD will take me up. Teach me thy way, O LORD, and lead me in a plain path, because of mine enemies. Deliver me not over unto the will of mine enemies: for false witnesses are risen up against me, and such as breathe out cruelty. I had fainted, unless I had believed to see the goodness of the LORD in the land of the living. Wait on the LORD: be of good courage, and he shall strengthen thine heart: wait, I say, on the LORD.
(Psalms 27:1-14 KJV)

Devotional Day 11

Let all bitterness, and wrath, and anger, and clamour, and evil speaking, be put away from you, with all malice: And be ye kind one to another, tenderhearted, forgiving one another, even as God for Christ's sake hath forgiven you. (Ephesians 4:31-32 KJV)

Knock it off...

We who are born again and full of the Holy Spirit are different from others, or at least we should be. There are things from the past that we drag with us when we come to Christ that prevent us from growing.

Those things are what affect our testimony in front of others. Many people do not believe in Jesus because many Christians show bad testimonies in their jobs, and with their family and friends.

You can not serve Christ and keep acting that way, so knock it off. I know it takes time to stop bad habits. The time that it takes is the time that we spend alone with Jesus.

Pray on this day for God to change your old way of acting and to renew you with His Holy Spirit. Let us be more like Jesus and less like our old selves.

Israel Hernández

Day 12

Who is like God?

Of all the things we can choose to trust only God never fails. He is good and His love for us is infinite and unconditional. We are His special creation, the apple of His eye.

We tend to put our trust in men, in something natural, but the problem is that we all fail. There is a portion of evil in each of us that we must fight against every day and we are not capable of doing or saying the right thing in every situation. At times we all will disappoint even those we love the most.

But God is different. He is always available to us and able to meet all our needs. He guides us, comforts us, protects us, provides for us, and gives us peace and joy. We are the ones who fail Him by not trusting Him, by disobeying, and by forgetting to spend time with Him.

There is no one like our God. There is no one else who can save, heal, and restore. I know there are people who are looking for something other than God because they do not know Him. But there is no one else. Only God.

Prayer for Today

My God, I love You so much and I know that there is no one like you. Today I put all my trust in You and only in You. Help me to be strong in You and to remain in Your presence. In the name of Jesus. Amen.

Biblical Reading of the Day

Philippians 4:1-23

Paul and Timotheus, the servants of Jesus Christ, to all the saints in Christ Jesus which are at Philippi, with the bishops and deacons: Grace be unto you, and peace, from God our Father, and from the Lord Jesus Christ. I thank my God upon every remembrance of you, Always in every prayer of mine for you all making request with joy, For your fellowship in the gospel from the first day until now; Being confident of this very thing, that he which hath begun a good work in you will perform it until the day of Jesus Christ: Even as it is meet for me to think this of you all, because I have you in my heart; inasmuch as both in my bonds, and in the defence and confirmation of the gospel, ye all are partakers of my grace. For God is my record, how greatly I long after you all in the bowels of Jesus Christ. And this I pray, that your love may abound yet more and more in knowledge and in all judgment; That ye may approve things that are excellent; that ye may be sincere and without offence till the day of Christ; Being filled with the fruits of righteousness, which are by Jesus Christ, unto the glory and praise of God. But I would ye should understand, brethren, that the things which happened unto

me have fallen out rather unto the furtherance of the gospel; So that my bonds in Christ are manifest in all the palace, and in all other places; And many of the brethren in the Lord, waxing confident by my bonds, are much more bold to speak the word without fear. Some indeed preach Christ even of envy and strife; and some also of good will: The one preach Christ of contention, not sincerely, supposing to add affliction to my bonds: But the other of love, knowing that I am set for the defence of the gospel. What then? notwithstanding, every way, whether in pretence, or in truth, Christ is preached; and I therein do rejoice, yea, and will rejoice. For I know that this shall turn to my salvation through your prayer, and the supply of the Spirit of Jesus Christ, According to my earnest expectation and my hope, that in nothing I shall be ashamed, but that with all boldness, as always, so now also Christ shall be magnified in my body, whether it be by life, or by death. For to me to live is Christ, and to die is gain. But if I live in the flesh, this is the fruit of my labour: yet what I shall choose I wot not. For I am in a strait betwixt two, having a desire to depart, and to be with Christ; which is far better:
(Philippians 1:1-23 KJV)

Devotional Day 12

There is therefore now no condemnation to them which are in Christ Jesus, who walk not after the flesh, but after the Spirit.
(Romans 8:1 KJV)

Why do you keep condemning yourself?

What we have done in the past has been left behind. Yes, we are not proud of our past but it was a past without God and if we did not have God in our lives then there is no need to be surprised that we sinned.

If we repented of our sins and gave our hearts to Jesus, all these sins were forgiven, washed and forgotten by our heavenly Father.

Do not let the enemy remind you how bad you were or how terrible your past was. Remind him of who you are today and who lives in you. We walk in the Spirit and not in the flesh, we have overcome by the blood of the Lamb.

When negative thoughts and condemnation come, rebuke them in the name of Jesus. And if someone says "but you are..." referring to your past, you will say "I was" now Christ lives in me, I am a new creation!

Israel Hernández

The Lord is at the door

Today we will talk about something that is too often ignored, the second coming of the Lord. But before Jesus comes in His power and glory to establish His kingdom, before He rules the nations and allows us to rule with Him, the rapture will come.

Are you waiting for that moment? Are you eagerly anticipating His return? In Revelation 22, John writes of this in the very last sentence of the Bible.

He that beareth witness of these things saith, Surely I come quickly. Amen; yes, come, Lord Jesus. Revelation 22:20

Those of us who love the Lord long for His coming. There is nothing in this world that binds us because we love Jesus more than anything else. But we have to live our lives worthy of the Lord, every day.

And what about your family? I hope you are doing the best

you can to bring them to the knowledge of Jesus. We have to have passion for the coming of the Lord and a sense of urgency for the day of rapture. There is not much time.

Prayer for Today

Heavenly Father, thank You for one more day and for sustaining me during the fast. Help me to live with a constant awareness that Your son Jesus will soon return. I want to live for You and do what You have called me to do. In the name of Jesus. Amen.

Biblical Reading of the Day

Luke 18:1-43

And he spake a parable unto them to this end, that men ought always to pray, and not to faint; Saying, There was in a city a judge, which feared not God, neither regarded man: And there was a widow in that city; and she came unto him, saying, Avenge me of mine adversary. And he would not for a while: but afterward he said within himself, Though I fear not God, nor regard man; Yet because this widow troubleth me, I will avenge her, lest by her continual coming she weary me. And the Lord said, Hear what the unjust judge saith. And shall not God avenge his own elect, which cry day and night unto him, though he bear long with them? I tell you that he will avenge them speedily. Nevertheless when the Son of man cometh, shall he find faith on the earth? And he spake this parable unto certain which trusted in themselves that they were righteous, and despised others: Two men went up into the temple to pray; the one a Pharisee, and the other a publican. The Pharisee stood and prayed thus with himself, God, I thank thee, that I am not as other men are, extortioners, unjust, adulterers, or even as this publican. I fast twice in the week, I give tithes of all that I possess. And the publican, standing afar off, would not lift up so much as his eyes unto heaven, but smote upon his breast, saying, God be merciful to me a sinner. I tell you, this man went down to his house justified rather than the other: for every one that exalteth himself shall be abased; and he that humbleth himself shall be exalted. And they brought unto him also infants, that he would touch them: but when his disciples saw it, they rebuked them. But Jesus called them unto him, and said, Suffer little children to come unto me, and forbid them not: for of such is the kingdom of God. Verily I say unto you, Whosoever shall not receive the kingdom of God as a little child shall in no wise enter therein. And a certain ruler asked him, saying, Good Master, what shall I do to inherit eternal life? And Jesus said unto him, Why callest thou me good? none is good, save one, that is, God. Thou knowest the commandments, Do not commit adultery, Do not kill, Do not steal, Do not bear false witness, Honour thy father and thy mother. And he said, All these have I kept from my youth up. Now when Jesus heard these things, he said unto him, Yet lackest thou one thing: sell all that thou hast, and distribute unto the poor, and thou shalt have treasure in heaven: and come, follow me. And when he heard this, he was very sorrowful: for he was very rich. And when Jesus saw that he was very sorrowful, he said, How hardly shall they that have riches enter into the kingdom of God! For it is easier for a camel to go through a needle's eye, than for a rich man to enter into the kingdom of God. And they that heard it said, Who then can be saved? And he said, The things which are impossible with men are possible with God. Then Peter said, Lo, we have left all, and followed thee. And he said unto them, Verily I say unto you, There is no man that hath left house, or parents, or brethren, or wife, or children, for the kingdom of God's sake, Who shall not receive

manifold more in this present time, and in the world to come life everlasting. Then he took unto him the twelve, and said unto them, Behold, we go up to Jerusalem, and all things that are written by the prophets concerning the Son of man shall be accomplished. For he shall be delivered unto the Gentiles, and shall be mocked, and spitefully entreated, and spitted on: And they shall scourge him, and put him to death: and the third day he shall rise again. And they understood none of these things: and this saying was hid from them, neither knew they the things which were spoken. And it came to pass, that as he was come nigh unto Jericho, a certain blind man sat by the way side begging: And hearing the multitude pass by, he asked what it meant. And they told him, that Jesus of Nazareth passeth by. And he cried, saying, Jesus, thou Son of David, have mercy on me. And they which went before rebuked him, that he should hold his peace: but he cried so much the more, Thou Son of David, have mercy on me. And Jesus stood, and commanded him to be brought unto him: and when he was come near, he asked him, Saying, What wilt thou that I shall do unto thee? And he said, Lord, that I may receive my sight. And Jesus said unto him, Receive thy sight: thy faith hath saved thee. And immediately he received his sight, and followed him, glorifying God: and all the people, when they saw it, gave praise unto God.
(Luke 18:1-43 KJV)

Devotional Day 13

And these signs shall follow them that believe; In my name shall they cast out devils; they shall speak with new tongues; They shall take up serpents; and if they drink any deadly thing, it shall not hurt them; they shall lay hands on the sick, and they shall recover.
(Mark 16:17-18 KJV)

How many believe?

Sadly, most believers do not experience the power of the Holy Spirit. Mostly this is because they have not been taught that He still moves powerfully.

Sometimes what is taught is that only the pastor can pray for the sick and we have to bring them to church. That is not what the Word teaches, even more, it is against the Word.

Jesus told us that the signs will follow "those who believe". Not that they will follow only the apostles, or only the leaders, but everyone who believes. The Holy Spirit is the one who works miracles, not the pastor and not us.

If you believe, everything Jesus says that you can do, you can do. You do not have to wait until Sunday to pray for your companions or family. Pray right now, in the same place and in the same moment that you are asked for prayer. If you believe God can work through you, He will.

Day 14

Week Two

Today is week two of fasting and only one more week is left. Looking back it seemed you would never make it but the Lord has sustained you. It is good to know that when we try to please God, He will support us.

Think about who you were two weeks ago and who you are today. Through the Holy Spirit you have left behind things of the past like bad habits, condemnation, and depression. Awareness of these changes will help you and motivate you to continue fasting until the 21st day.

Meditate on what you still need to surrender to God. What is inside of you that slows you down and prevents you from growing spiritually. What sin are you keeping that you have not given to God to be forgiven.

No matter how bad our past has been, all our sins are forgiven if we surrender them to Jesus in repentance. Today present your sins before God and decide to leave behind your grief, guilt and condemnation.

Prayer for Today

Our Father, thank You for Your support during these weeks that I have fasted. Help me to finish this last week in victory. Your Word has been bread for me. Help me to leave all my past behind. In the name of Jesus. Amen.

Biblical Reading of the Day

James 1:1-27

James, a servant of God and of the Lord Jesus Christ, to the twelve tribes which are scattered abroad, greeting. My brethren, count it all joy when ye fall into divers temptations; Knowing this, that the trying of your faith worketh patience. But let patience have her perfect work, that ye may be perfect and entire, wanting nothing. If any of you lack wisdom, let him ask of God, that giveth to all men liberally, and upbraideth not; and it shall be given him. But let him ask in faith, nothing wavering. For he that wavereth is like a wave of the sea driven with the wind and tossed. For let not that man think that he shall receive any thing of the Lord. A double minded man is unstable in all his ways. Let the brother of low degree rejoice in that he is exalted: But the rich, in that he is made low: because as the flower of the grass he shall pass away. For the sun is no sooner risen with a burning heat, but it withereth the grass, and the flower thereof falleth, and the grace of the fashion of it perisheth: so also shall the rich man fade away in his ways. Blessed is the man that endureth temptation: for when he is tried, he shall

receive the crown of life, which the Lord hath promised to them that love him. Let no man say when he is tempted, I am tempted of God: for God cannot be tempted with evil, neither tempteth he any man: But every man is tempted, when he is drawn away of his own lust, and enticed. Then when lust hath conceived, it bringeth forth sin: and sin, when it is finished, bringeth forth death. Do not err, my beloved brethren. Every good gift and every perfect gift is from above, and cometh down from the Father of lights, with whom is no variableness, neither shadow of turning. Of his own will begat he us with the word of truth, that we should be a kind of firstfruits of his creatures. Wherefore, my beloved brethren, let every man be swift to hear, slow to speak, slow to wrath: For the wrath of man worketh not the righteousness of God. Wherefore lay apart all filthiness and superfluity of naughtiness, and receive with meekness the engrafted word, which is able to save your souls. But be ye doers of the word, and not hearers only, deceiving your own selves. For if any be a hearer of the word, and not a doer, he is like unto a man beholding his natural face in a glass: For he beholdeth himself, and goeth his way, and straightway forgetteth what manner of man he was. But whoso looketh into the perfect law of liberty, and continueth therein, he being not a forgetful hearer, but a doer of the work, this man shall be blessed in his deed. If any man among you seem to be religious, and bridleth not his tongue, but deceiveth his own heart, this man's religion is vain. Pure religion and undefiled before God and the Father is this, To visit the fatherless and widows in their affliction, and to keep himself unspotted from the world.
(James 1:1-27 KJV)

Devotional Day 14

My soul followeth hard after thee: thy right hand upholdeth me.
(Psalms 63:8 KJV)

Your hand upholds me

In His Word the Lord always gives us what we need to be victorious. There are no special revelations for some ministers who then pass them on to only a few believers. Everything God wants you to do and not do is in the Word.

The Lord sustains you with His right hand. That is a promise that is for everyone. But read this verse carefully, there is something we must do before receiving His promise. In this case, we have to follow very close to Him.

There are no blessings without obedience. We have already said many times in this fast that we must remain in the Lord. We should not just ask for what we need when we need it. But we must keep a direct communication with God at all times, spend time alone with Him, and remain in His Word.

Look at this example: You have a friend for years, and suddenly he stops talking to you, he no longer calls you or looks for you, and when you look for him he ignores you. Suddenly, after a few years he comes to you just to ask you for money or a favor that will cost you a lot. You give it to him, and then he disappears for a while, until he needs something from you again. How will you feel?

This is how God feels when we only seek Him from time to time because we need something from Him. The relationship between you and God must be maintained every day without fail and everything you need will be given to you.

Day 15

He is the King

Our God and Savior is the King of all creation. There is no one or anything that compares with Him. By His Word all things were created and without Him nothing would exist.

God gave us authority over all creation. When we chose to sin we gave our authority up and became slaves to the devil. Because of our choice God has allowed the dominion of the enemy to be established for a time in this world.

But God provided a way to save us from the power and consequence of sin. Jesus. He took our sin, paid our price, died in our place, was resurrected into glorious life, and has all power and authority. And because He did this for us, when we become one with Him, we have the same righteousness and authority. Now Christians, those of us who have been born again, have authority over every fallen angel and every devil. Although we can still be tempted, we cannot be forced to sin.

Start to act as part of the kingdom of God on earth because we will soon reign with Jesus. Walk with authority and not with fear because He is the one in control of all things.

Prayer for Today

Lord, thank You because You have given me authority over the world of darkness and I need not fear. Help me understand that You are King of kings and You are in control of all things. In the name of Jesus. Amen.

Biblical Reading of the Day

Mark 8:1-38

In those days the multitude being very great, and having nothing to eat, Jesus called his disciples unto him, and saith unto them, I have compassion on the multitude, because they have now been with me three days, and have nothing to eat: And if I send them away fasting to their own houses, they will faint by the way: for divers of them came from far. And his disciples answered him, From whence can a man satisfy these men with bread here in the wilderness? And he asked them, How many loaves have ye? And they said, Seven. And he commanded the people to sit down on the ground: and he took the seven loaves, and gave thanks, and brake, and gave to his disciples to set before them; and they did set them before the people. And they had a few small fishes: and he blessed, and commanded to set them also before them. So they did eat, and were filled: and they took up of the broken meat that was left seven baskets. And they that had eaten were about four thousand: and he sent them away. And straightway he entered into a ship with his disciples, and came into the parts of Dalmanutha. And the Pharisees came forth, and began to question with him, seeking of him a sign from heaven, tempting him. And he sighed deeply in his spirit, and saith, Why doth this generation seek after a sign? verily I say unto you, There shall no sign be given unto this generation. And he left them, and entering into the ship again departed to the other side. Now the disciples had forgotten to take bread, neither had they in the ship with them more than one loaf. And he charged them, saying, Take heed, beware of the leaven of the Pharisees, and of the leaven of Herod. And they reasoned among themselves, saying, It is because we have no bread. And when Jesus knew it, he saith unto them, Why reason ye, because ye have no bread? perceive ye not yet, neither understand? have ye your heart yet hardened? Having eyes, see ye not? and having ears, hear ye not? and do ye not remember? When I brake the five loaves among five thousand, how many baskets full of fragments took ye up? They say unto him, Twelve. And when the seven among four thousand, how many baskets full of fragments took ye up? And they said, Seven. And he said unto them, How is it that ye do not understand? And he cometh to Bethsaida; and they bring a blind man unto him, and besought him to touch him. And he took the blind man by the hand, and led him out of the town; and when he had spit on his eyes, and put his hands upon him, he asked him if he saw ought. And he looked up, and said, I see men as trees, walking. After that he put his hands again upon his eyes, and made him look up: and he was restored, and saw every man clearly. And he sent him away to his house, saying, Neither go into the town, nor tell it to any in the town. And Jesus went out, and his disciples, into the towns of Caesarea Philippi: and by the way he asked his disciples, saying unto them, Whom do men say that I am? And they answered, John the Baptist: but some say, Elias; and others, One of the prophets. And he saith unto them, But whom say ye that I am? And Peter answereth and saith unto him, Thou art the Christ. And he charged them that they should tell no man of him. And he began to teach them, that the Son of man must suffer many things, and be rejected of the elders, and of the chief priests, and scribes, and be killed, and after three days rise again. And he spake that saying openly. And Peter took him, and began to rebuke him. But when he had turned about and looked on his disciples, he rebuked Peter, saying, Get thee behind me, Satan: for thou savourest not the things that be of God, but the things that be of men. And when he had called the people unto him with his disciples also, he said unto them, Whosoever will come after me, let him deny himself, and take up his cross, and follow me. For whosoever will save his life shall lose it; but whosoever shall lose his life for my sake and the gospel's, the same shall save it. For what shall it profit a man, if he shall gain the whole world, and lose his own soul? Or what shall a man give in exchange for his soul? Whosoever therefore shall be ashamed of me and of my words in this adulterous and sinful generation; of him also shall the Son of man be ashamed, when he cometh in the glory of his Father with the holy angels. (Mark 8:1-38 KJV)

Devotional Day 15

But be ye doers of the word, and not hearers only, deceiving your own selves. (James 1:22 KJV)

Do you listen but do not do?

There are many who listen to the Word on Sundays in church and then forget about it. During the week there is no memory of what God spoke to them during the service.

There are also others who are scholars of the Word. They study the scriptures and memorize many biblical passages, they even teach others what the Bible says, but they do not do what they teach.

But that's not the way we are, is it? We listen to the Word, we read and meditate on it, and we put it into practice. There is a conviction in our hearts when we see in the scriptures that there is something we should be doing that we are not.

Your love and your faith in Jesus is demonstrated by obeying His Word. Therefore it is necessary to be doers and not only hearers. There is no greater satisfaction than doing the will of God and living in obedience. This will please God.

Remember that it is fasting and prayer

I congratulate you for having come this far in this fast. I know that it has been a great blessing for you and your spiritual life. It will only take five more days to finish the fast so we will finish strong.

This time you have dedicated to God is not just a time without eating. We must maintain a life of continuous prayer with God. Prayer is very important in order to know Jesus and to know the plan He has for your life.

Knowing how to listen to His voice through His Word and through the Holy Spirit will help us to win in spiritual warfare. We cannot forget to spend time alone with God, neither now nor after the fast.

This week you will end up increasing your prayer time. Did you know that Daniel prayed three times a day? Let's do the same and spend time with the Lord.

Prayer for Today

Father, thank You for this beautiful day that You created for me. Today I ask You to help me spend more time alone with Jesus. I need more of You. In the name of Jesus. Amen.

Biblical Reading of the Day

Mark 9:1-50

And he said unto them, Verily I say unto you, That there be some of them that stand here, which shall not taste of death, till they have seen the kingdom of God come with power. And after six days Jesus taketh with him Peter, and James, and John, and leadeth them up into an high mountain apart by themselves: and he was transfigured before them. And his raiment became shining, exceeding white as snow; so as no fuller on earth can white them. And there appeared unto them Elias with Moses: and they were talking with Jesus. And Peter answered and said to Jesus, Master, it is good for us to be here: and let us make three tabernacles; one for thee, and one for Moses, and one for Elias. For he wist not what to say; for they were sore afraid. And there was a cloud that overshadowed them: and a voice came out of the cloud, saying, This is my beloved Son: hear him. And suddenly, when they had looked round about, they saw no man any more, save Jesus only with themselves. And as they came down from the mountain, he charged them that they should tell no man what things they had seen, till the Son of man were risen from the dead. And they kept that saying with themselves, questioning one with another what the rising from the dead should mean. And they asked him, saying, Why say the scribes that Elias must first come? And he answered and told them, Elias verily cometh first, and restoreth all things; and how it is written of the Son of man, that he must suffer many things, and be set at nought. But I say unto you, That Elias is indeed come, and they have done unto him whatsoever they listed, as it is written of him. And when he came to his disciples, he saw a great multitude about them, and the scribes questioning with them. And straightway all the people, when they beheld him, were greatly amazed, and running to him saluted him. And he asked the scribes, What question ye with them? And one of the multitude answered and said, Master, I have brought unto thee my son, which hath a dumb spirit; And wheresoever he taketh him, he teareth him: and he foameth, and gnasheth with his teeth, and pineth away: and I spake to thy disciples that they should cast him out; and they could not. He answereth him, and saith, O faithless generation, how long shall I be with you? how long shall I suffer you? bring him unto me. And they brought him unto him: and when he saw him, straightway the spirit tare him; and he fell on the ground, and wallowed foaming. And he asked his father, How long is it ago since this came unto him? And he said, Of a child. And ofttimes it hath cast him into the fire, and into the waters, to destroy him: but if thou canst do any thing, have compassion on us, and help us. Jesus said unto him, If thou canst believe, all things are possible to him that believeth. And straightway the father of the child cried out, and said with tears, Lord, I believe; help thou mine unbelief. When Jesus saw that the people came running together, he rebuked the foul spirit, saying unto him, Thou dumb and deaf spirit, I charge thee, come out of him, and enter no more into him. And the spirit cried, and rent him sore, and came out of him: and he was as one dead; insomuch that many said, He is dead. But Jesus took him by the hand, and lifted him up; and he arose. And when he was come into the house, his disciples asked him privately, Why could not we cast him out? And he said unto them, This kind can come forth by nothing, but by prayer and fasting. And they departed thence, and passed through Galilee; and he would not that any man should know it. For he taught his disciples, and said unto them, The Son of man is delivered into the hands of men, and they shall kill him; and after that he is killed, he shall rise the third day. But they understood not that saying, and were afraid to ask him. And he came to Capernaum: and being in the house he asked them, What was it that ye disputed among yourselves by the way? But they held their peace: for by the way they had disputed among themselves, who should be the greatest. And he sat down, and called the twelve, and saith unto them, If any man desire to be first, the same shall be last of all, and servant of all. And he took a child, and set him in the midst of them: and when he had taken him in his arms, he said unto them, Whosoever shall receive one of such children in my name, receiveth me: and whosoever shall receive me, receiveth not me, but him that sent me. And John answered him, saying, Master, we saw one casting out devils in thy name, and he followeth not us: and we forbad him, because he followeth not us. But Jesus said, Forbid him not: for there is no man which shall do a miracle in my name, that can lightly speak evil of me. For he that is not against us is on our part. For whosoever shall give you a cup of water to drink in my name, because ye belong to Christ, verily I say unto you, he shall not lose his reward. And whosoever shall offend one of these little ones that believe in me, it is better for him that a millstone were

hanged about his neck, and he were cast into the sea. And if thy hand offend thee, cut it off: it is better for thee to enter into life maimed, than having two hands to go into hell, into the fire that never shall be quenched: Where their worm dieth not, and the fire is not quenched. And if thy foot offend thee, cut it off: it is better for thee to enter halt into life, than having two feet to be cast into hell, into the fire that never shall be quenched: Where their worm dieth not, and the fire is not quenched. And if thine eye offend thee, pluck it out: it is better for thee to enter into the kingdom of God with one eye, than having two eyes to be cast into hell fire: Where their worm dieth not, and the fire is not quenched. For every one shall be salted with fire, and every sacrifice shall be salted with salt. Salt is good: but if the salt have lost his saltness, wherewith will ye season it? Have salt in yourselves, and have peace one with another.
(Mark 9:1-50 KJV)

Devotional Day 16

For with God nothing shall be impossible. (Luke 1:37 KJV)

What is your impossible?

In life we have things or situations that we want to change. Things that take away our joy and peace Maybe your marriage is collapsing because of the other person and you don't how it can be fixed.

For others, the impossible is a disease that has no cure or that keeps appearing again and again. Maybe it's an addiction that has you trapped. Maybe alcoholism is breaking your relationships or maybe its drugs, sexual addiction or depression.

But I have news for you, for God there is nothing impossible. And some will say "that is for God not for me". If that is your thinking you are wrong. If you trust in God and abide in Him, you can do everything in Christ who strengthens you.

It is not because of your strength, remember Christ lives in you and if so, the power of the Holy Spirit that dwells within you can break ALL chains that bind you. The time to cry and get depressed is over, the time to give in to temptation is over. It is time to stay in God and let Him break the impossible of your life. He can do everything! If you allow Him...

Day 17

The attacks will come but He is greater

The enemy does not like to see you in spiritual victory, your joy, your peace and your closeness to God bother him. He is looking for the moment when you lower your guard, for an opportunity to attack.

But there is no reason to fear if we remain in Jesus and in His Word. The Lord is a shield around us, our rock of salvation. In Him is the source of life and peace that surpasses all understanding.

When spiritual attacks come just rebuke and declare the Word. If the enemy's darts penetrate, it is because a door is opened. In some way you have disobeyed, ask God to reveal it to you. All you have to do is repent and leave sin behind.

Nothing can harm us while we are in the fold. But the wolf is out waiting to devour the one who leaves. The good Shepherd protects us, so remain in His presence.

Prayer for Today

Lord and Father, I thank You for being my sustenance and my Pastor. In Your presence I am safe and nothing will harm me. Help me to remain in Your fold and to dwell under the shadow of Your wings. In the name of Jesus. Amen.

Biblical Reading of the Day

Isaiah 41:1-29

Keep silence before me, O islands; and let the people renew their strength: let them come near; then let them speak: let us come near together to judgment. Who raised up the righteous man from the east, called him to his foot, gave the nations before him, and made him rule over kings? he gave them as the dust to his sword, and as driven stubble to his bow. He pursued them, and passed safely; even by the way that he had not gone with his feet. Who hath wrought and done it, calling the generations from the beginning? I the LORD, the first, and with the last; I am he. The isles saw it, and feared; the ends of the earth were afraid, drew near, and came. They helped every one his neighbour; and every one said to his brother, Be of good courage. So the carpenter encouraged the goldsmith, and he that smootheth with the hammer him that smote the anvil, saying, It is ready for the sodering: and he fastened it with nails, that it should not be moved. But thou, Israel, art my servant, Jacob whom I have chosen, the seed of Abraham my friend. Thou whom I have taken from the ends of the earth, and called thee from the chief men thereof, and said unto thee, Thou art my servant; I have chosen thee, and not cast thee away. Fear thou not; for I am with thee: be not dismayed; for I am thy God: I will strengthen thee; yea, I will help thee; yea, I will uphold thee with the right hand of my righteousness. Behold, all they that were incensed against thee shall be ashamed and confounded: they shall be as nothing; and they that strive with thee shall perish. Thou shalt seek them, and shalt not find them, even them that contended with thee: they that war against thee shall be as nothing, and as a thing of nought. For I the LORD thy God will hold thy right hand, saying unto thee, Fear not; I will help thee. Fear not, thou worm Jacob, and ye men of Israel; I will help thee, saith the LORD, and thy redeemer, the Holy One of Israel. Behold, I will make thee a new sharp threshing instrument having teeth: thou shalt thresh the mountains, and beat them small, and shalt make the hills as chaff. Thou shalt fan them, and the wind shall carry them away, and the whirlwind shall scatter them: and thou shalt rejoice in the LORD, and shalt glory in the Holy One of Israel. When the poor and needy seek water, and there is none, and their tongue faileth for thirst, I the LORD will hear them, I the God of Israel will not forsake them. I will open rivers in high places, and fountains in the midst of the valleys: I will make the wilderness a pool of water, and the dry land springs of water. I will plant in the wilderness the cedar, the shittah tree, and the myrtle, and the oil tree; I will set in the desert the fir tree, and the pine, and the box tree together: That they may see, and know, and consider, and understand together, that the hand of the LORD hath done this, and the Holy One of Israel hath created it. Produce your cause, saith the LORD; bring forth your strong reasons, saith the King of Jacob. Let them bring them forth, and shew us what shall happen: let them shew the former things, what they be, that we may consider them, and know

the latter end of them; or declare us things for to come. Shew the things that are to come hereafter, that we may know that ye are gods: yea, do good, or do evil, that we may be dismayed, and behold it together. Behold, ye are of nothing, and your work of nought: an abomination is he that chooseth you. I have raised up one from the north, and he shall come: from the rising of the sun shall he call upon my name: and he shall come upon princes as upon morter, and as the potter treadeth clay. Who hath declared from the beginning, that we may know? and beforetime, that we may say, He is righteous? yea, there is none that sheweth, yea, there is none that declareth, yea, there is none that heareth your words. The first shall say to Zion, Behold, behold them: and I will give to Jerusalem one that bringeth good tidings. For I beheld, and there was no man; even among them, and there was no counsellor, that, when I asked of them, could answer a word. Behold, they are all vanity; their works are nothing: their molten images are wind and confusion.
(Isaiah 41:1-29 KJV)

Devotional Day 17

For we have not an high priest which cannot be touched with the feeling of our infirmities; but was in all points tempted like as we are, yet without sin.
(Hebrews 4:15 KJV)

He knows what you're going through

The Lord Jesus is no stranger to the temptations you face every day. He was tempted in everything, that is, whatever temptation you may have He had, but He never gave in. He never sinned.

Being tempted does not mean that our spiritual life is not right. Quite the opposite. Those of us who are really Christians, born again and filled with the Holy Spirit, face many temptations because we are a threat to the kingdom of darkness.

What we do with temptation is what makes the difference. When we are tempted, if we put our strength and willpower against it, or if we try to reason with it, we will probably fall. Temptations are to be rebuke with the Word immediately.

We can sin within our mind, this is where spiritual warfare occurs. Do not let any sinful thoughts dwell in your mind because they are doors into which the enemy can enter. Overcome temptation with the Word. Jesus taught us how to do it.

Day 18

How to hear the voice of God

God spoke face to face with Moses in a unique way. But even though we may not experience it in the exact same way, God keeps talking to us today. The problem is we often do not realize it.

There are different ways in which God speaks to us. The most common, though not the only way, is through His Word. Not only is everything that we need to know written, but in specific moments, the Word we need is made alive in us.

God also speaks through people. Many times the Lord uses people to answer our prayers. Not only can God use someone to bless us, to supply a material need, but also to speak to us.

God speaks through His ministers. The Lord uses a pastor to speak to His people. Not only to the body in general, but also to you in specific. But beware of those "prophets" who like to invent things and love to say "God told me". Test everything that people tell you is from God against the Word of God.

There are many examples in which God speaks to His children. There is not simply one way in which God communicates with us, He does as he wants. Just be persistent and attentive in prayer and surely the answer will come.

Prayer for Today

Lord, thank You for being an accessible God and for giving me access to Your presence through the blood of Jesus. Teach me to listen to Your voice and to discern when a strange voice tries to talk to me. In the name of Jesus. Amen.

Biblical Reading of the Day

Psalm 34:1-22

A Psalm of David, when he changed his behaviour before Abimelech; who drove him away, and he departed. I will bless the LORD at all times: his praise shall continually be in my mouth. My soul shall make her boast in the LORD: the humble shall hear thereof, and be glad. O magnify the LORD with me, and let us exalt his name together. I sought the LORD, and he heard me, and delivered me from all my fears. They looked unto him, and were lightened: and their faces were not ashamed. This poor man cried, and the LORD heard him, and saved him out of all his troubles. The angel of the LORD encampeth round about them that fear him, and delivereth them. O taste and see that the LORD is good: blessed is the man that trusteth in him. O fear the LORD, ye his saints: for there is no want to them that fear him. The young lions do lack, and suffer hunger: but they that seek the LORD shall not want any good thing. Come, ye children, hearken unto me: I will teach you the fear of the LORD.

What man is he that desireth life, and loveth many days, that he may see good? Keep thy tongue from evil, and thy lips from speaking guile. Depart from evil, and do good; seek peace, and pursue it. The eyes of the LORD are upon the righteous, and his ears are open unto their cry. The face of the LORD is against them that do evil, to cut off the remembrance of them from the earth. The righteous cry, and the LORD heareth, and delivereth them out of all their troubles. The LORD is nigh unto them that are of a broken heart; and saveth such as be of a contrite spirit. Many are the afflictions of the righteous: but the LORD delivereth him out of them all. He keepeth all his bones: not one of them is broken. Evil shall slay the wicked: and they that hate the righteous shall be desolate. The LORD redeemeth the soul of his servants: and none of them that trust in him shall be desolate.

(Psalms 34:1-22 KJV)

Devotional Day 18

If we confess our sins, he is faithful and just to forgive us our sins, and to cleanse us from all unrighteousness.
(1 John 1:9 KJV)

Do not hide your sins

Who can hide something from God? The Lord knows everything we do, no matter who else sees it. It does not matter that we did it in the privacy of our room, or what we threw in the bag when nobody was watching. God sees everything.

He already knows our sins but we have to confess them before God to have them forgiven. When we confess we agree with God that what we did was wrong. Confessing our sins is something we should do daily.

It is not necessary to go to the minister and confess everything we have done wrong. But in some instances confessing to another christian will help us break the chains that bind us. This is when we should seek pastoral counseling.

God is willing to forgive our sins and cleanse us from all unrighteousness. All we have to do is confess what He already knows. Isn't that easy? He already knows.

Israel Hernández

Day 19

Fill yourself with the things of God

Two days are left to finish the fast and we must be filled with more of the Lord. During these 19 days you have read the Word every day, something many have never done before. You have listened to only Christian music during these days.

Also during this fast, you have prayed and read devotionals daily. You have learned to meditate on the Word of God and learned to leave condemnation and guilt behind. You have filled yourself with God more than ever before.

I know that what you have done for the Lord has changed your life and caused you to grow spiritually. God is doing the same thing for you that He has done for me. What else can you give to the Lord? What is the next thing we will do to fill ourselves with Jesus?

Maybe the Lord is asking you to give up the things that take you away from Him. Maybe it's time to stop watching TV shows that do not honor God. Maybe those friendships that do nothing but tempt you to backslide have got to go.

Now is the time to increase your relationship with God. It is time to stand firm in your house and declare that your house will serve the Lord. The fast is almost over but your relationship with God should be stronger than ever before. Fasting breaks the desires of the flesh and removes all immorality from you. Fill yourself with God so that there is no room for sinful desires. Fill yourself with God.

Prayer for Today

Dear Father, I thank You for what You have shown me and what You have taught me. Today I am close to You and tomorrow I want to be closer. I want to be filled with more of You and with Your Word, help me Lord. In the name of Jesus. Amen.

Biblical Reading of the Day

John 2:1-25

And the third day there was a marriage in Cana of Galilee; and the mother of Jesus was there: And both Jesus was called, and his disciples, to the marriage. And when they wanted wine, the mother of Jesus saith unto him, They have no wine. Jesus saith unto her, Woman, what have I to do with thee? mine hour is not yet come. His mother saith unto the servants, Whatsoever he saith unto you, do it. And there were set there six waterpots of stone, after the manner of the purifying of the Jews, containing two or three firkins apiece. Jesus saith unto them, Fill the waterpots with water. And they filled them up to the brim. And he saith unto them, Draw out now, and bear unto the governor of the feast. And they bare it. When the ruler of the feast had tasted the water that was made wine, and knew not whence it was: (but the servants which drew the water knew;) the governor of the feast called the bridegroom, And saith unto him, Every man at the beginning doth set forth good wine; and when men have well drunk, then that which is worse: but thou hast kept the good wine until now. This beginning of miracles did

Jesus in Cana of Galilee, and manifested forth his glory; and his disciples believed on him. After this he went down to Capernaum, he, and his mother, and his brethren, and his disciples: and they continued there not many days. And the Jews' passover was at hand, and Jesus went up to Jerusalem, And found in the temple those that sold oxen and sheep and doves, and the changers of money sitting: And when he had made a scourge of small cords, he drove them all out of the temple, and the sheep, and the oxen; and poured out the changers' money, and overthrew the tables; And said unto them that sold doves, Take these things hence; make not my Father's house an house of merchandise. And his disciples remembered that it was written, The zeal of thine house hath eaten me up. Then answered the Jews and said unto him, What sign shewest thou unto us, seeing that thou doest these things? Jesus answered and said unto them, Destroy this temple, and in three days I will raise it up. Then said the Jews, Forty and six years was this temple in building, and wilt thou rear it up in three days? But he spake of the temple of his body. When therefore he was risen from the dead, his disciples remembered that he had said this unto them; and they believed the scripture, and the word which Jesus had said. Now when he was in Jerusalem at the passover, in the feast day, many believed in his name, when they saw the miracles which he did. But Jesus did not commit himself unto them, because he knew all men, And needed not that any should testify of man: for he knew what was in man. (John 2:1-25 KJV)

Devotional Day 19

For a day in thy courts is better than a thousand. I had rather be a doorkeeper in the house of my God, than to dwell in the tents of wickedness. (Psalms 84:10 KJV)

There is no better place

When we learn to dwell in the presence of God we understand that there is no better place. The best place is where we feel so close to Him that we can almost touch Him.

But it's not that we must travel in the spiritual to where God is because He dwells in us through the Holy Spirit. When we are alone with Him in prayer and adoration, His presence becomes more real and palpable.

There is no place in this world better than being in Him. No activity that this world offers compares to basking in His presence and, sadly, most people choose activities that lead to destruction and not to edification.

"Everything is lawful for me, but everything does not profit me," the apostle Paul said. No one can tell you what to do or where to go, but if the places you frequent take you away from God, why frequent them? Choose what is best.

Israel Hernández

Keep praying

Prayer is an important part of our relationship with God, perhaps the most important. In a relationship it is vital that both parties maintain honest and open communication.

Do not try to hide things you did in the past or when you are thinking things that are not from God. Confess everything in front of your heavenly Father and He will forgive it all.

Now, God wants to hear from your lips everything that is in your heart and your mind but He also wants you to listen to Him. In this we fail a lot. We talk and we talk, we ask, we complain and we cry but we do not want to, or maybe we do not know how to, listen.

Take time today to hear the voice of God. During your time alone with God, remain silent and listen. Maybe He will speak to you in your heart or in the Word, perhaps through devotionals but He will always answer you.

Prayer for Today

Heavenly Father, thank You for giving me the blessing of communicating with You. I want to hear Your voice and know Your will. Help me to get closer to You. In the name of Jesus. Amen.

Biblical Reading of the Day

Matthew 28:1-20

In the end of the sabbath, as it began to dawn toward the first day of the week, came Mary Magdalene and the other Mary to see the sepulchre. And, behold, there was a great earthquake: for the angel of the Lord descended from heaven, and came and rolled back the stone from the door, and sat upon it. His countenance was like lightning, and his raiment white as snow: And for fear of him the keepers did shake, and became as dead men. And the angel answered and said unto the women, Fear not ye: for I know that ye seek Jesus, which was crucified. He is not here: for he is risen, as he said. Come, see the place where the Lord lay. And go quickly, and tell his disciples that he is risen from the dead; and, behold, he goeth before you into Galilee; there shall ye see him: lo, I have told you. And they departed quickly from the sepulchre with fear and great joy; and did run to bring his disciples word. And as they went to tell his disciples, behold, Jesus met them, saying, All hail. And they came and held him by the feet, and worshipped him. Then said Jesus unto them, Be not afraid: go tell my brethren that they go into Galilee, and there shall they see me. Now when they were going, behold, some of the watch came into the city, and shewed unto the chief priests all the things that were done. And when they were assembled with the elders, and had taken counsel, they gave large money unto the soldiers, Saying, Say ye, His disciples came by night, and stole him away while we slept. And if this come to the governor's ears, we will persuade him, and secure you. So they took the money, and did as they were taught: and this saying is commonly reported among the Jews until this day. Then the eleven disciples went away into Galilee, into a mountain where Jesus had appointed them. And when they saw him, they worshipped him: but some doubted. And Jesus came and spake unto them, saying, All power is given unto me in heaven and in earth. Go ye therefore, and teach all nations, baptizing them in the name of the Father, and of the Son, and of the Holy Ghost: Teaching them to observe all things whatsoever I have commanded you: and, lo, I am with you alway, even unto the end of the world. Amen.

(Matthew 28:1-20 KJV)

Devotional Day 20

Jesus said unto him, Thou shalt love the Lord thy God with all thy heart, and with all thy soul, and with all thy mind.
(Matthew 22:37 KJV)

Love Him with everything

The first commandment that the Lord gave to us is to love Him. Not only to love Him, but to love Him with all your mind, with all your heart and with all your strength.

It is not enough to spend one hour with Him each Sunday and forget about Him the rest of the time. There are many people who say they love God but do not make Him part of their life.

Everything we do in this fast are things we should be doing anyway. Use it as a spiritual recharge and continue seeking God with all your strength.

One important thing about the first commandment is that if we really come to love God as He asks us to love Him, that love will allow us to obey the other nine commandments. Ask God to help you to love Him as He wants you to love Him. We can only love Him as He deserves through the power of the Holy Spirit.

Israel Hernández

Day 21

The answer is near

Today is the last day of this 21-day fast. Looking back it seemed very difficult at the start but now that you have reached the goal it seems that you could continue for 10 more days. But that was not what God called you to do.

Today, meditate on what you have learned during these three weeks. Think about how your spiritual life was before you started, what didn't you do before that is now part of your routine. Think of the times (if applicable) that you missed during fasting, whether eating, or not praying, or not meditating on the Word.

Start thinking about what you would do differently next time to keep yourself completely focused on God. Also take time today to plan what you will do starting tomorrow.

When you break the fast this afternoon, thank God for being your sustenance and your helper. Pray for your family, friends, your pastors, and for all those who, with a sincere heart, seek to please God. Also pray for me.

Now that we have finish this fast together, I encourage you to continue the "fast but with eating". What does that mean? That you eat but everything else that you did during the fast you keep doing every day. Keep praying morning and night, keep listening to Christian music, read the Word daily, meditate on the Word, create your own devotionals and share them with others, praise and worship the Lord with songs.

My prayer is that each of you live a life of victory in spiritual warfare. May the attacks of the enemy and of our own flesh that occur in our minds and in our hearts be overcome. May you be filled with the fullness of God and may rivers of living water flow from within you.

And may the Lord bless you
May the Lord keep you
May the Lord make his face shine upon
you and have mercy on you
May the Lord turn his face towards you
And give you (Shalom) peace, grace, favor and the fullness of
God. In the name of Jesus. Amen.

Prayer for Today

My beloved Father, thank you for being my bread, my peace and my strength during this fast. Today I am closer to You than yesterday and tomorrow I want to be even closer. Help me to walk with You and live for You. I ask You to dress me with all the armor of God and guide me wherever You want me to go. I love You so much more than yesterday. In the name of Jesus. Amen.

Biblical Reading of the Day

Revelation 22:1-21

And he shewed me a pure river of water of life, clear as crystal, proceeding out of the throne of God and of the Lamb. In the midst of the street of it, and on either side of the river, was there the tree of life, which bare twelve manner of fruits, and yielded her fruit every month: and the leaves of the tree were for the healing of the nations. And there shall be no more curse: but the throne of God and of the Lamb shall be in it; and his servants shall serve him: And they shall see his face; and his name shall be in their foreheads. And there shall be no night there; and they need no candle, neither light of the sun; for the Lord God giveth them light: and they shall reign for ever and ever. And he said unto me, These sayings are faithful and true: and the Lord God of the holy prophets sent his angel to shew unto his servants the things which must shortly be done. Behold, I come quickly: blessed is he that keepeth the sayings of the prophecy of this book. And I John saw these things, and heard them. And when I had heard and seen, I fell down to worship before the feet of the angel which shewed me these things. Then saith he unto me, See thou do it not: for I am thy fellowservant,

and of thy brethren the prophets, and of them which keep the sayings of this book: worship God. And he saith unto me, Seal not the sayings of the prophecy of this book: for the time is at hand. He that is unjust, let him be unjust still: and he which is filthy, let him be filthy still: and he that is righteous, let him be righteous still: and he that is holy, let him be holy still. And, behold, I come quickly; and my reward is with me, to give every man according as his work shall be. I am Alpha and Omega, the beginning and the end, the first and the last. Blessed are they that do his commandments, that they may have right to the tree of life, and may enter in through the gates into the city. For without are dogs, and sorcerers, and whoremongers, and murderers, and idolaters, and whosoever loveth and maketh a lie. I Jesus have sent mine angel to testify unto you these things in the churches. I am the root and the offspring of David, and the bright and morning star. And the Spirit and the bride say, Come. And let him that heareth say, Come. And let him that is athirst come. And whosoever will, let him take the water of life freely. For I testify unto every man that heareth the words of the prophecy of this book, If any man shall add unto these things, God shall add unto him the plagues that are written in this book: And if any man shall take away from the words of the book of this prophecy, God shall take away his part out of the book of life, and out of the holy city, and from the things which are written in this book. He which testifieth these things saith, Surely I come quickly. Amen. Even so, come, Lord Jesus. The grace of our Lord Jesus Christ be with you all. Amen.
(Revelation 22:1-21 KJV)

Devotional Day 21

I will instruct thee and teach thee in the way which thou shalt go: I will guide thee with mine eye.
(Psalms 32:8 KJV)

He takes care of you

The Lord did not create us and put us in this world only to abandon us and leave us lost in this world. It would be impossible to find the path on which we must walk if we had to find it by ourselves.

Our God shows us the way we should walk so that we do not get lost. And more than that, He sent His only begotten Son to teach us, by example.

Not only that, He is so good and loves us so much that He also has His eyes on us so that when we take the wrong path, we can return. How good is God! He not only speaks to us and guides us, He also accompanies us through His Holy Spirit.

Israel Hernández

ABOUT THE AUTHOR

Pastor Israel Hernandez has been serving the Lord for more than fifteen years in different facets. Preacher in several churches in Puerto Rico and the United States, in Spanish as well as in English. He also served as a Pastoral Counselor in the Ministry of Health and Evangelism in his home church. He also preached in various institutions and churches on his beloved island of Puerto Rico. He currently works at Knowing Jesus Ministry in the state of Michigan, USA.

Contact: contacto@mcajesus.com
734-883-5823

23735219R00076

Made in the USA
Columbia, SC
13 August 2018